Making the Case for Minimum Expectations

Michael A. MacDonald

Copyright © 2009 Michael A. MacDonald
All rights reserved.

ISBN: 1-4392-5497-4
ISBN-13: 9781439254974

Visit www.booksurge.com to order additional copies.

Contents

Acknowledgments v

Chapter 1   Introduction 1

Chapter 2   The Dr. George F. Mack Middle School 5

Chapter 3   The Birth of *Minimum Expectations* 7

Chapter 4   *Minimum Expectations* 11
                 The Dr. George F. Mack Middle School Program

Chapter 5   Results 17

Chapter 6   *Minimum Expectations* in Elementary School . . 27

Chapter 7   *Minimum Expectations* in the High School . . . 31

Chapter 8   Final Thoughts 35

About the Author 37

Acknowledgments

Many people provided inspiration for the creation of the *Minimum Expectations* program as well as the encouragement to write this book. Having a faculty of educators that are devoted to student learning and willing to stand up and voice their concerns is one of the best gifts a principal could have. In particular, I would like to thank Matt Chambers for his annual venting and wishing that we could do more to minimize student apathy in our 8th grade students. It was that type of concern that pushed me to search out a solution. I also have to give a heartfelt thank you to Diane Meredith for being such a guiding light of encouragement as well as providing her editing and knowledge to any and all of my professional undertakings.

As a result of being encouraged to present the program to the DCMO BOCES Instructional Support Services Principal meeting by Kerrie Johnston there are multiple schools implementing the *Minimum Expectations* program. Thank you, Kerrie.

It is a pleasure to work for a district that maintains a vision that student learning is the highest priority year after year. With the addition of the support needed to create and maintain successful programs like *Minimum Expectations* we can make a huge impact on student learning.

Finally, I thank my family for their continued support and understanding throughout my career.

Chapter 1
Introduction

Rigor, Relevance, Assessments, Aligned Curriculum… key concepts in education today. It is undeniable that without these instructional elements, students will not receive the education they require and deserve. However, despite the ever-growing, ever-changing body of knowledge around school improvement and increased student achievement, one variable remains constant: students need to complete assignments to be successful. The success of the education of each student weighs heavily on the student's effort applied to the learning process. The key area for the application of that effort is in the completion of assignments.

There is much debate over the worth of homework in education. In our current public education system, homework is a much-needed aspect of learning when the assignment is based on developing skill or increasing knowledge in a specific content area. Teachers have voiced frustration for decades over the inability to get many students to complete assignments. They have claimed that students would be successful in passing assessments and ultimately their courses if they would put in the required effort needed to complete the assignments appropriately and on time.

Since entering administration in 1997, a recurring frustration was being voiced throughout the middle and high school students. Students that were struggling were not completing assignments and a solution was not in sight. Student learning has been my primary focus as a building principal. After moving to the middle school in 2003, the same frustration continued to be voiced by staff members. I began studying and investigating practices that could be implemented in our rural district. In the spring of 2006 I was approached by a veteran teacher who was extremely frustrated with the apathy of his current eighth graders. This was a recurring discussion every spring for many years. "If we could only get them to do their work", "We need to come with some way", etc. This year was different. Having recently reviewed material from a presentation by Richard DuFour as well as an article published in the April 2006 Educational Leadership Journal entitled <u>Leading Adolescents to Mastery</u>, I was ready to attempt to put a program in place. The model sprouted from the key concepts of current educational leaders. Richard DuFour spoke of a "hovering" concept using study hall monitors. Make students find it easier to comply and complete assignments rather than have a study hall monitor hover over them daily. Rick Wormeli spoke of the meaning of accepting a student is not turning in an assignment and giving the student a zero. I recall the statement, "How can an assignment be worth giving if it's ok for students not to complete it? Must be it wasn't important to their learning". I recall Mike Schmoker making the same point with the reference of the use of a "crayola curriculum" in elementary education. It was time to take a chance and make a difference.

The development of the program began with an open-invitation faculty/staff discussion at the end of the school year following a memo sent to all staff addressing all concerns and comments received. The discussion lasted over thirty minutes and resulted in a building wide commitment to the piloting of a program of "minimum expectations". In early August, the traditional staff information packet was mailed, this packet included a draft of the program guidelines for implementation in September. The program has been *tweaked* each year based on staff discussions and suggestions.

The goal of this book is to make a case for setting minimum expectations for your students' completion of assignments. We will move through a review of the current program in place at the Dr. George F. Mack Middle School, the results of the program, and a case for an extension of the program from Kindergarten through grade 10.

Chapter 2
The Dr. George F. Mack Middle School

The Dr. George F. Mack Middle School is one of three schools in the Walton School District in a beautiful, rural town in Upstate New York. Major industry in the area includes farming, bluestone mining, and several factories within a thirty-minute commute. The free and reduced percentage is approximately fifty percent, and the special education percentage approximately twenty percent (fluctuating annually).

The middle school houses grades six through eight with average class sizes of eighty students. The program is centered on character education with a well-established advisor program and daily grade level teaming sessions. The bell schedule is a traditional nine-period schedule with thirty-six minute class periods. The facility is attached to the HS complex and shares the cafeteria, auditorium and staff members in the areas of Physical Education, Art, Music, Languages Other Than English, Technology, Health, and Family and Consumer Sciences.

Chapter 3
The Birth of *Minimum Expectations*

As mentioned in the *Introduction*, a veteran teacher approached me in the spring of 2006 to vent frustration on the beginning of the annual eighth grade student apathy. Being as attuned to the topic as I was at the time, I was ready to attempt to put something in place to ease teacher frustration and our growing student apathy problem. The challenge was to create a program that would have an academic benefit but would not be another time-consuming task for teachers to integrate in a class period that was already lacking for time. Of course, the key to any initiative is to gain the consensus and ownership/buy in of the staff. The next three months were spent obtaining all of the thoughts the staff had to offer, from concerns over students not being held responsible if we *force* them to do their assignments to ideas of how to format the program; every piece of input was valued and reviewed for relevance.

The process began with an initial memo sent to all staff. The memo asked for responses to the following questions:
1. *Do you support holding students to a minimum expectation on all assignments? (Tests & quizzes not included.)*
2. *What do you feel the minimum expectation should be (eg. 75%)?*
3. *What are your thoughts regarding the process?*

The memo was accompanied with information on an article regarding a school that had implemented a *no zero* policy, and the goal was to elicit ideas and concerns from each staff member's reflection on the article.

The next step was to review and reflect on the responses received from the staff. The information was compiled, and the following information was returned to staff for their review and reflection.

WHAT ARE WE TRYING TO ASSESS? WHAT IS A GRADE POINT AVERAGE COMPRISED OF?

1. Test and Quizzes – Direct Assessment Data
2. Homework, Projects (papers, group, research, etc.)
3. Class Participation

2 and 3 are the areas of focus for 98% of this process in order to teach responsibility and work ethic. Test and quizzes will be addressed only if a student fails to complete the assessment.

KEY QUESTIONS/CONCERNS
1. Level – 75%, 85%? Should it be different for each student?
2. Teacher dedication and commitment – will everyone put in the effort needed?
3. How do we give them the help needed to meet the expectation?
   - Mandatory Help
   - After School Study Club
   - Held on days without After School Study Club
   - Hardcore Case – Saturday Morning Detention
   - **If ability is the problem – move to Child Study (RTI); and explore issue; modify expectation if effort is there.**
4. Process – How will we hold students accountable in a manageable way?
5. Special Education – Some students' minimum expectation may need to be modified. Special Education teachers will assist with this.

Throughout this process there was a series of individual conversations and team level discussions about the initiative. The process climaxed with an open invitation discussion at the end of the year following a memo sent to all staff addressing all concerns and comments received. The discussion lasted over thirty minutes and ended with a building-wide commitment to the piloting of a program of "Minimum Expectations".

Chapter 4
Minimum Expectations... **The Dr. George F. Mack Middle School Program**

The goal of the program is to eliminate student apathy. A key component is the requirement that students complete assignments at an individual quality level of 75% or higher (Fig.1). The value of 75% was a faculty decision based on the need to ensure students are working at a quality level that will ensure the retention of the material or skill the assignment is meant to produce. The concept of an <u>individual quality level</u> is essential for the differentiation of the expectations of students. Students with learning difficulties and learning disabilities may not be able to be held to the same expectations as other students. However, each student with a modified level of expectation must have an appropriate individualized education plan (IEP) in place or be referred to the response to intervention program (RTI) for evaluation.

Fig. 1
Minimum Expectations

PROCEDURE

1. Requirement of 75% or better "quality" work.
   a. Work" is defined as anything other than tests and quizzes. However, a student refusing or failing to complete a test or quiz cannot be ignored.
   b. "75%" or higher "quality": We have some situations that will necessitate "individualizing" what the "75% quality" means for the student. Those situations will be students who are in special education or in need of the child study program. Teaming will be a very important aspect of the program.
   c. Follow through: * There will be mandatory help scheduled at each grade level on activity days (refer to bell schedule Appendix pg.1). Students will need to be told that they have to attend and information on assignments to be completed, must be placed in the folder for the help period in the office.
      - Teachers of afternoon classes or "off help" day classes will send students to the office for them to call home to tell their parents they need to stay after school and the reason for it. Students will attend study club on days that it is available. Other days, we will provide teacher supervision as needed. Transportation could be a complicating factor on non-study club days.

The program is based on building responsibility and eliminating gaps in student learning due to their not completing assignments. When an assignment is completed in mandatory help, a reduced value of 65% is assigned upon successful completion. Students receive credit for completing the assignment rather than receiving a zero and not completing the assignment.

How does the program work? Homework is evaluated for completion at the beginning of the class period while students are performing a bell-ringer activity. If the student is found to not have the assignment or has an assignment that is obviously done below the expectation (yes, this is very obvious) the following sequence of events will occur:

The student is given a mandatory help pass (Fig. 2) and sent to the office to call his or her parent/guardian. Upon entering the office, the student informs the secretary what class he or she is calling for and is allowed to call. The secretary documents the student's name and teacher that sent the student to call in a log book while listening intently to the phone conversation. The secretaries play a very key role in the program. Many times students will attempt to fake a call to avoid actually speaking with a parent. A keen listener may pick this up and call back to ensure that the student did indeed speak with the parent. Students are required to tell the parent the assignment that they didn't complete and when they will be attending mandatory help (midday or after school).

Fig. 2

MANDATORY HELP

STUDENT'S NAME: _____
CLASS: _____
ASSIGNMENT: _____
_____

Please Circle One: **ACTIVITY TIME   AFTER SCHOOL**
PROCEDURE:
Call Parent, informing them of what assignment was not completed.
Place form in Mandatory Help File. If parent tells student they cannot stay, turn form in to Mrs. Webler for Mr. MacDonald to call parent.

Midday mandatory help is scheduled during our version of recess. It occurs every other day opposite the lunch period. If a student is assigned, he/she will attend for the entire period. If the assignment(s) are not completed at the end of the period, the student will be sent back to the office to call a parent and inform him/her that the student will now need to stay after school to finish what he/she was unable to finish during the midday session. If a student refuses to work or fails to attend the student is referred for discipline.

After-school mandatory help is held daily. Students assigned are required to attend for the length of time (up to an hour) it takes to complete the assignment. Transportation is provided on Tuesdays and Thursdays. If students require transportation on either day they are required to remain in the help room for the full hour. On the remaining days of the week, transportation is the responsibility of the parent. Of course, there are occasions when a student can't stay due to a lack of transportation or a family obligation. If such a situation arises, the student is instructed to speak with the Principal and a phone call may be made to the parent. Students are required to show the Principal the completed assignment first thing the next day. If a student doesn't attend or refuses to work he/she is referred for discipline. The reasoning behind holding students only as long as is needed to complete the assignment is to build responsibility, showing the student that it is easier to just complete the assignment that took just fifteen minutes and walk home with friends or go to practice on time. Figure 3 depicts a quick reference guide for the *Mandatory Help* process of the *Minimum Expectation* program provided to staff in the August mailing as well as in staff folders opening day of each year.

Fig. 3   **Dr. George F. Mack Middle School**
2007 -2008

MANDATORY HELP PROCEDURE

Activity Day	*Non-Activity Day*
1. Assigned to Mandatory Help or (if not completed)	1. Advisor (if activity permits) or
2. Call Parent–Stay after school	2. Call Parent–Stay after school

Student receives full credit or reduced (65% for the completed assignment).

The following are issues and/or situations that have brought forward concerns:

1. Student fails to attend mandatory help and work is not completed
   a. Our procedure:
      i. Student is disciplined for cutting an assigned class (referral to Vice Principal).
      ii. Student is required to complete the assignment (receives a 50%).
2. Student attends mandatory help but fails to finish assignments
   a. Our Procedure:
      i. Student is disciplined for insubordination (referral to Vice Principal).

ii. Student is required to complete the assignment (receives a 50%).

Each situation will still need to be approached on a case-by-case basis. Teachers are asked to use compassion and a respectful approach with students.

Chapter 5
Results

The goal of *Minimum Expectations* is to eliminate student apathy. The reality is that it does just that for the majority of the students. For those that continue to struggle with meeting the expectations, it allows for the implementation of additional interventions. The program gives us the ability to obtain clarity regarding whether a student is struggling due to ability or effort and allows for an accurate approach to intervention. Additionally, the utilization of the log-entry data can assist with the development of a system of interventions including parental conferences, RTI referral, and behavioral management.

From the beginning of the program the results having been entirely positive and include the following:
- Retention rates are at an all-time low. Second year of implementation yielded a 100% promotion rate. Third year is showing the same positive results.

- Summer school attendance is focused on actual student skill development rather than a punitive element centered on student apathy.
- Parent involvement and communication has increased. Students call the day that an assignment is not completed, which results in immediate feedback for parents. Parent conferences have been scheduled earlier in the school year, allowing more time for improvement. Again, the ability to separate student apathy from skill deficit allows for a more productive and beneficial parental meeting and potential partnership.
- Quarterly results are revealing 58-62% of the student body with GPAs of 84.5% or higher with the highest percentage in each grade level scoring at above 90%.
- Resource Room providers have the ability to focus on current assignments and student needs rather than continually focus on work that is overdue.
- Quality versus quantity assignments. The theory of having to assign a high quantity of assignments in an attempt to ensure skill development for all students is not relevant. This allows assignments to be of higher quality and increased rigor.

The following graphs highlight significant grade distribution data in specific courses. Instructional methods play a significant role in the level of impact *Minimum Expectations* will have on student achievement.

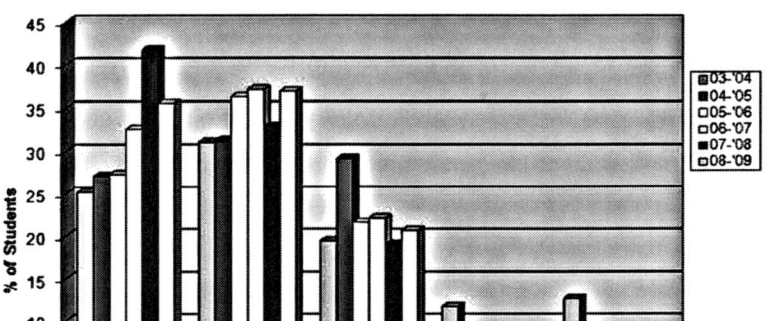

There is a significant shift in student results since the implementation of 2006-2007. The 7th grade science teacher methods include unit packets for guided notes and assignments. Student apathy was a significant cause of more than five percent of students failing each year. *Minimum Expectations* not only resulted in an immediate decrease in students failing but also resulted in a significant increase in the number of students achieving above 90%.

7th Grade Social Studies Grade Distribution '03/'04 - '08/'09

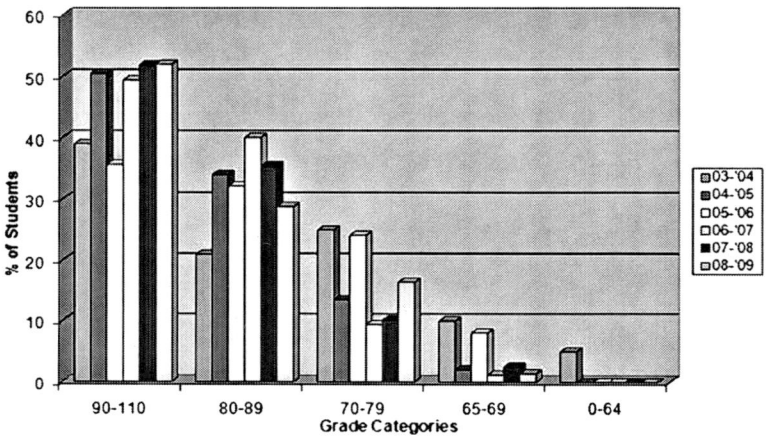

The 7th grade social studies results show a consistency in student results that was not present prior to the implementation of *Minimum Expectations*. Significant change is present in the 65-69% and the 90-110% range.

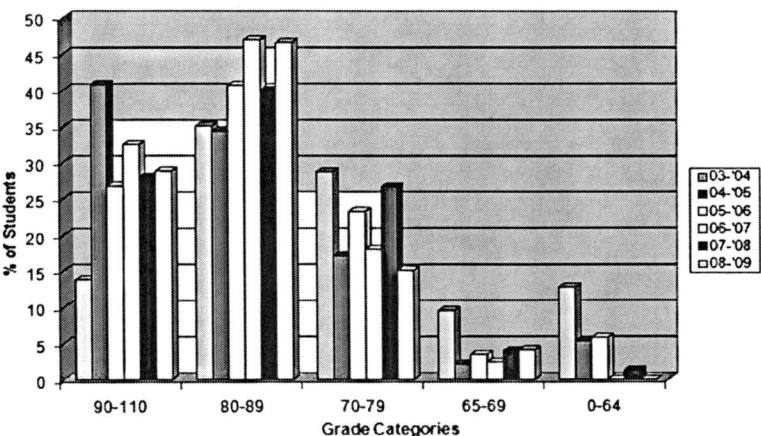

The 7th grade math results show a significant and consistent reduction in the 0-64% range.

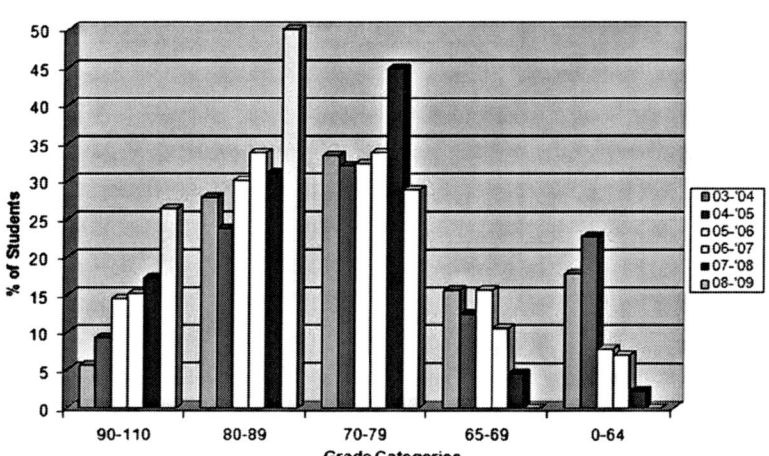

8th Grade Science Grade Distribution '03/'04 - '08/'09

8th grade science has shown very significant results since the implementation of *Minimum Expectations*. There continues to be significant reductions in the 0-64% and the 0-69% range. In addition, there continues to be consistence increases in the 80-89% and 90-110% range. Student apathy was a significant factor in student results prior to the 2006-2007 school year.

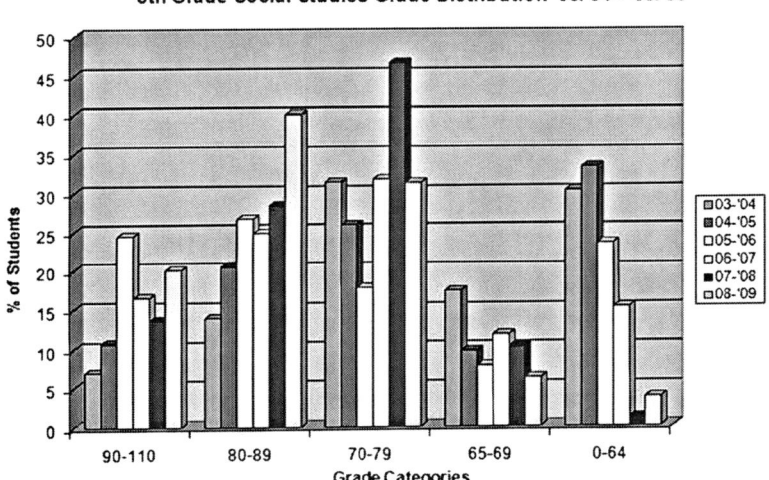

8th grade social studies has shown the most significant change in student results. The results have shown a decrease from a consistent above 30% to a consistent below 5% in the 0-64% range. In addition, results in the 80-89% range are showing a consistent improvement.

New York State assessments serve as another source of data when evaluating the effectiveness of a school improvement program. The significant data is shown below in a series of charts provided by Broome Tioga BOCES. All assessments are indicating a significant improvement in student achievement after the implementation year of *Minimum Expectations* (2006-07)

26 | Making the Case for Minimum Expectations

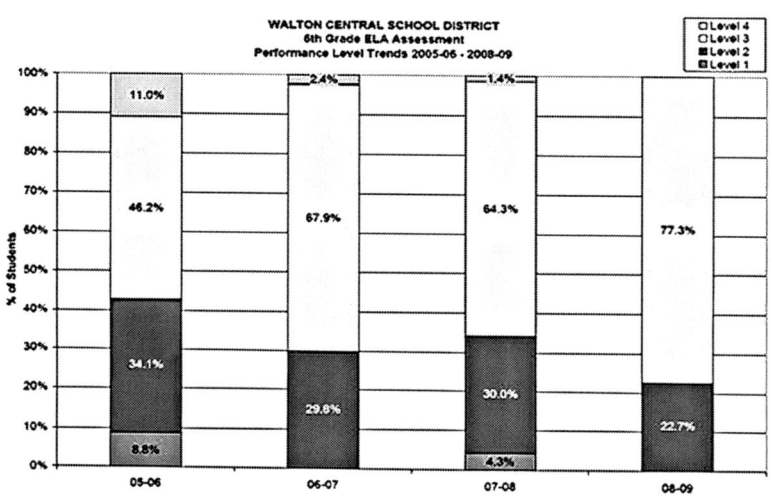

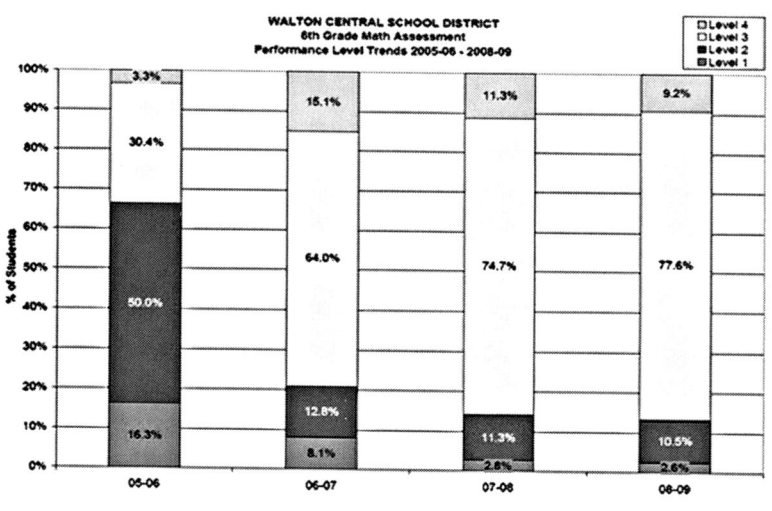

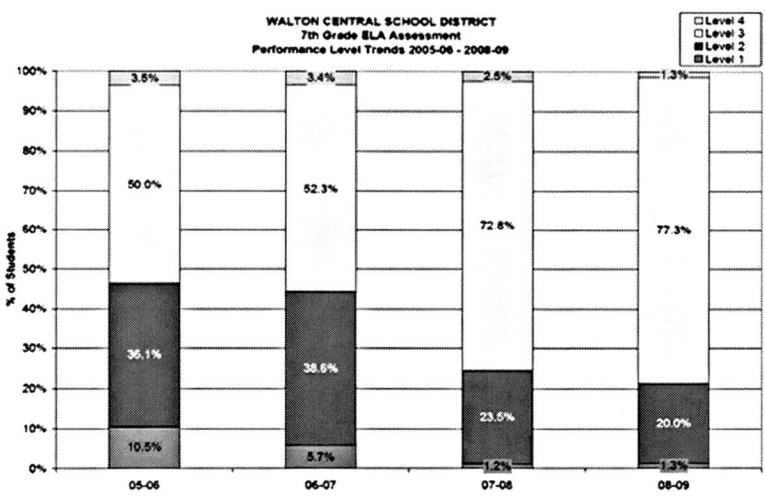

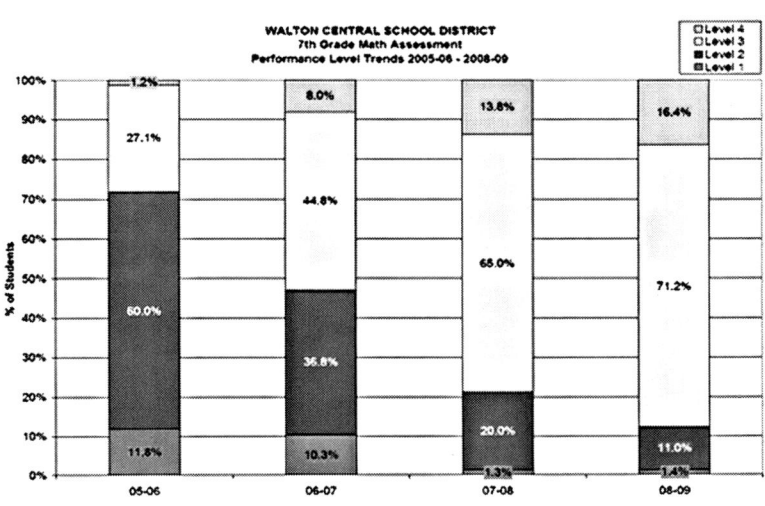

Making the Case for Minimum Expectations

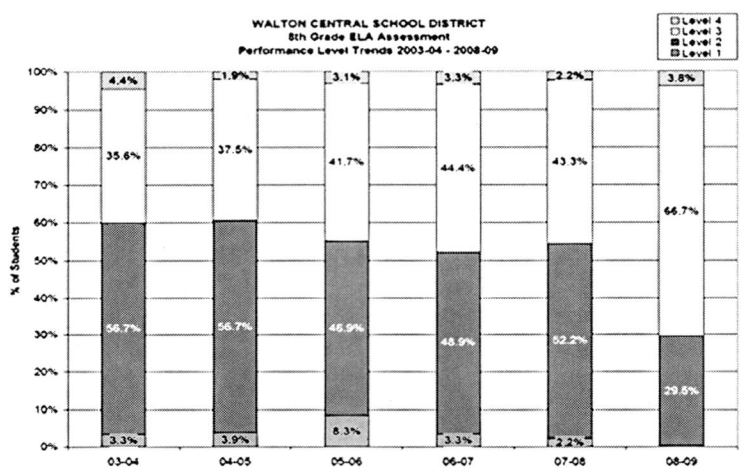

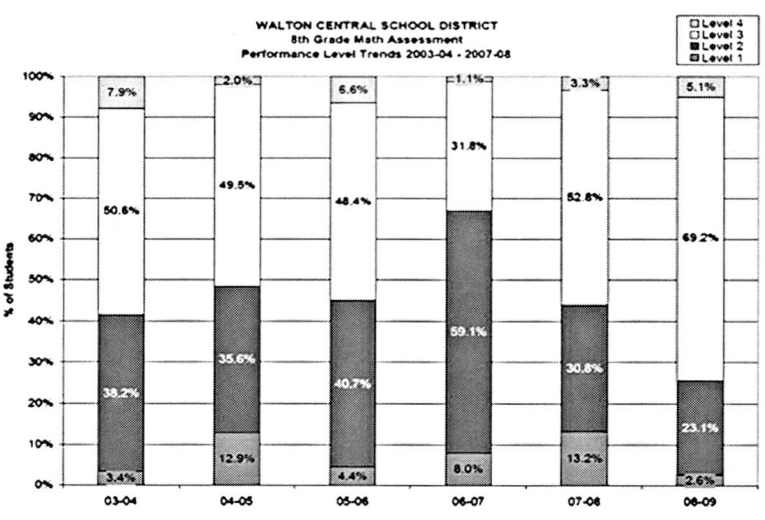

Chapter 6
Minimum Expectations **in Elementary School**

The typical elementary school has an informal *Minimum Expectations* program. If a student fails to complete an assignment, he/she is held during recess to finish the assignment. This has been a policy that has proven to be successful over time. The reason? Students realize that it is easier to do the assignment than miss out on a portion of the recess period. The benefit of such a policy is limited by the lack of formality and parental involvement. While parents are much more attentive to the education program when their child is young, they are also in a learning and growing period as a parent. There is a tremendous opportunity to educate and train parents as to the importance of students' completing assignments at a high-quality level. The majority of parents expect their children to be able to handle the responsibility of school by the time they reach middle school. Unfortunately, in many cases neither the parent nor the student is prepared for the responsibility.

From the time students enter Kindergarten they should be held to *Minimum Expectations*. If the expectation is that a document is signed and returned to school, and the parent fails to do so, contact should be made. Contact can be in the form of a reminder note. If the issue of the parent not following through on obligations continues, then there should be a progression of interventions ranging from additional notes to a phone call to a conference. No, Kindergarten is not too soon to implement a program and begin training parents and students on how to be responsible.

When students begin to receive homework assignments, it is imperative that there be a system of parental contact in place. Students are receiving homework at a younger and younger age. Parents are busier and busier in life, and unfortunately some things are determined to be a low priority. In many cases it is the assignment. A system of contact with parents, coupled with a clear school-wide intervention system, puts the assignments back at a high priority level. As students mature, the parental contact should shift from notes home to students' being responsible for the parental contact. A first level may be to have the students write the note to the parent explaining that they didn't complete their assignment and why it is important that they complete all assignments on time and with their best effort. Helping a student with the explanation is an excellent way to educate him/her as to the importance of completing assignments, it drives home the point that students will not be allowed to choose to fail. Beginning in the upper grades, students can begin calling their parents. It is incredibly powerful to have students call their parents at work or home and tell them that they didn't complete an assignment.

Introducing a program of *Minimum* Expectations at the elementary level will prevent those hardened habits that sometimes are created by years of being allowed to choose not to do an assignment. Students need to know that failure is not an option and that the first step toward failure is to not complete an assignment. We care too much to let that happen. Those small gaps in learning that develop from not completing assignments over the elementary years becoming larger and larger as students enter middle school and then move on to high school.

Chapter 7
Minimum Expectations in the High School

Having spent seven years working in a high school, I know exactly what will be said in every high school when discussing the merit of a *Minimum Expectations* program. The theme will be that when a student gets to high school, he/she needs to be responsible for his/her own learning. Teachers will teach and students will make a decision as to whether they want to learn or not. If they don't.... well the choice was theirs. Think about those statements for a moment. We are talking about thirteen, fourteen, and fifteen year olds. Have you ever spent any time with a student of this age? They can't think past the current day, let alone what the implications of not doing assignments will have in the future. These are students who can't drive, vote, or quit school. Why? Because they are not responsible to make such choices. However, we will allow them to make the choice to fail. Doesn't sound quite right ... does it?

Now to be fair, I must say that there is a time for students to take responsibility for their learning. I just don't believe we can expect 9th and 10th grade students to be ready to handle such responsibility. We need an intervention program in place for those two grade levels. When I review the grades of the freshmen who have left the *Minimum Expectations* program, those students who are struggling are being allowed to not do their assignments. They are starting off the school year doing very well but then are beginning to revert to the old habits when they realize that the only accountability is the assignment of a zero for the assignment not completed. 9th and 10th grade are such important years in the careers of our students. We can't afford to allow them to lose credit and fail courses due to not being held accountable for assignments, and therefore not meeting the expectation of the teacher.

A *Minimum Expectations* program in the high school should be aligned with the middle school to ensure an easy transition. However, the program should be scaled back as students move from 9th to 10th grade. The 9th grade program should consist of parental phone calls and students being held during a mid-day free time period (if applicable) as well as after school. The program should also include a tiered intervention system based on the data obtained from call logs maintained in the office. 10th grade should show a shift in the responsibility to the student. That may consist of not having students call their parent but continuing to assign students to the help session and held accountable if they don't attend and complete the assignment. Again, a tiered intervention system should be in place to ensure the student receives the interventions needed to be successful. Following 10th grade, students need to begin to exhibit the responsibility required to be successful in college, work, or the military. This does not minimize the need for interventions. However, the interventions will be quite different and will be focused on parental contact and possible loss of privileges.

It is very important to remember that we are trying to put capable and responsible young adults into the world. Allowing students to build habits of mediocrity and poor work ethic will not allow them to be successful. All too often our frustrations cloud our overall purpose.

Chapter 8
Final Thoughts

As a principal, I see hundreds of students and parents each year. I have the privilege of working with some of the most fantastic and intriguing individuals I have ever encountered. I am continually amazed and given a sense of hope by the quality of individuals that are entering the world after completing high school. I am also saddened and concerned over the number of students that are forced to grow up too fast, forced to face elements of life at a very young age that many of us adults have yet to face. These students are one of the main reasons I remain working in a school setting. They need all of us to help them grow and develop into capable young adults. I see students who struggle with academics due to having developed poor work ethics. Some of those students have too much on their plates at home and need an extended school day, which an after-school mandatory help room offers. Many of them need to know it is not a choice to do their homework and that yes, we do care about them and their futures. They need us.

Setting *Minimum Expectations* will help students. There is no argument with that statement. I am working in education to help students. Are you? If so, set the expectation ... hold them accountable ... they will not disappoint you!

About the Author

Michael MacDonald has been a substitute teacher, math teacher, special education teacher, vice principal, high school principal, and middle school principal. He began his education career in 1993 and has been working in the Walton Central School District throughout his career. He has been the principal of The Dr. George F. Mack since 2003 replacing his mentor, Jim Hoover upon his retirement.

Consultant service inquiries: mmacdonald08@yahoo.com